Surviving a Fire

by Heather Adamson

amicus readers

2

 amicus readers

Say hello to amicus readers.

You'll find our helpful dog, Amicus, chasing a ball—to let you know the reading level of a book.

A

 1

 2

Learn to Read
Frequent repetition of sentence structures, high frequency words, and familiar topics provide ample support for brand new readers. Approximately 100 words.

Read Independently
Repetition is mixed with varied sentence structures and 6 to 8 content words per book are introduced with photo label and picture glossary supports. Approximately 150 words.

Read to Know More
These books feature a higher text load with additional nonfiction features such as more photos, time lines, and text divided into sections. Approximately 250 words.

Amicus Readers are published by Amicus
P.O. Box 1329, Mankato, Minnesota 56002
www.amicuspublishing.us

Printed in the United States of America at at Corporate Graphics, in North Mankato, Minnesota.

Series Editor   Rebecca Glaser
Series Designer   Bobbi J. Wyss
Photo Researcher   Heather Dreisbach

Library of Congress Cataloging-in-Publication Data
Adamson, Heather, 1974-
  Surviving a fire / by Heather Adamson.
      p. cm. – (Amicus readers. Be prepared)
  Includes bibliographical references and index.
  Summary: "A level 2 Amicus Reader that discusses the dangers of house fires, how to prepare a fire escape plan, and how to get out during a fire and stay safe after the fire is out"–Provided by publisher.
  ISBN 978-1-60753-149-4 (library bound)
  1. Fire protection engineering–Juvenile literature.
  2. Fires–Juvenile literature. 3. Preparedness–Juvenile literature. I. Title.
  TH9148.A3323 2011
  613.6'9–dc22
                                              2011005588

Photo Credits
Vince Streano/GettyImages, Cover; Blue Shadows/Alamy, 1; TheImageArea/iStockphoto , 5; fireSafety.gov, 7, 20m; Erik Isakson/GettyImages, 8, 20b; Nick Kennedy/Alamy, 9, 20; Willie B. Thomas/iStockphoto, 10; WCephei/iStockphoto , 11, 21t; Ryan Ruffatti/iStockphoto, 12t, 21m; Jimmi Larsen/iStockphoto , 12b, 21b; © Blend Images/Alamy, 15; © Sang Lei I Dreamstime.com, 16l; manley099/iStockphoto, 16r; Detail Parenting/Alamy, 17; John Rich/iStockphoto, 19, 20t

1035   3-2011
10 9 8 7 6 5 4 3 2 1

Table of Contents

Fires 4

Be Prepared 6

During a Fire 12

After a Fire 18

Photo Glossary 20

Activity: Plan an Escape Path 22

Ideas for Parents and Teachers 23

Index and Web Sites 24

Fires

Fires can start anywhere from forests to homes and schools. Smoke, heat, and flames make fires dangerous. You can stay safe if you are prepared.

Be Prepared

Learn the fire **escape plans**
for your home and school so
you can get out fast. Most
rooms have two ways out.
One might be a window.
Learn how to open and climb
out the window safely.

escape plan

Fire drills let you pretend there is a fire and practice your fire escape plans. Listen carefully to directions during drills.

Besides practicing your ways out, plan a place to meet everyone outside. Then firefighters will know if anyone is still inside.

fire drill

Learn your address and what **emergency** number to call if you see a fire. Always plan to get out first and then call when you are safe.

Never try to put out a fire
yourself even if you have a
fire extinguisher.

fire extinguisher

During a Fire

Smoke detectors and fire alarms make loud noises to warn you of fires. When you hear the noise, use your escape plan.

Apartment buildings have **sprinkler systems**. Don't worry if you get wet or dirty. Just get out quickly.

smoke detector

sprinkler system

Stay calm if you are stuck in a fire. Get down low and cover your mouth to keep the smoke out. Don't hide from firefighters. They will help you get out safely.

If your hair or clothes catch on fire, stop, drop, and roll. Don't run. That can make flames bigger.

STOP

DROP

ROLL

Lie on the ground and roll back
and forth until the flames are out.
Get out if you can or wait calmly
to be rescued.

After a Fire

If you have burns or feel sick, you may need to go to the hospital. Don't go back into a burned building until an adult says it is ok. Fires can be scary, but knowing what to do keeps you safe.

19

Photo Glossary

emergency
a sudden and dangerous situation, such as a fire, that must be dealt with immediately

escape plan
a plan for getting out in a fire; escape plans should have two ways out and a meeting place

fire drill
a time to practice a fire escape plan, practicing how to get out of a building in case of fire

fire extinguisher
a device used to put
out fires

smoke detector
a machine that makes
a loud noise when it
senses smoke

sprinkler system
pipes or sprinklers in a
building that spray water
or foam to help put out fires

Activity: Plan an Escape Path

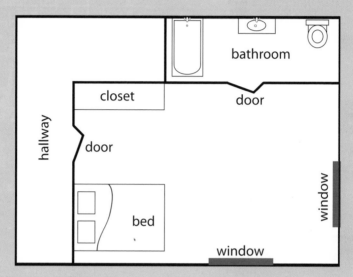

1. Trace or draw this bedroom floorplan onto a piece of paper. Mark a path for the best way out if there is a fire.

2. Now mark a different path out of the room.

Answers: Did you mark the door to the hallway? Did you mark the windows? They are good options for getting out. The doors to bathroom and the closet are not good choices. They don't lead to a way out.

Ideas for Parents and Teachers

amicus readers

Be Prepared, an Amicus Readers Level 2 series, provides simple explanations of what disasters are and offers reassuring steps that kids and families can take to prepare. As you read this book with your children or students, use the ideas below to help them get even more out of their reading experience.

Before Reading

* ✳ Read the title and ask the students if they've ever experienced a fire or know someone who has.

* ✳ Ask the students how they would know when there was a fire. Ask them why we need to be prepared for fires.

* ✳ Use the photo glossary words to help them predict what they will learn from the book.

Read the Book

* ✳ Ask the students to read the book independently.

* ✳ Provide support where necessary. Remind them to look up unfamiliar words in the picture glossary if they need help.

After Reading

* ✳ Ask the students to retell what they learned about fires and how to prepare for them. Compare their answers to what they said before reading the book.

* ✳ Have students do the activity on page 22 and talk about what the fire escape plan is in your home or school.

Index

burns 18
emergency number 10
escape plans 6
fire alarms 12
fire drills 8
fire extinguisher 11
firefighters 8, 14
flames 4, 16, 17
forests 4

homes 4, 6
meeting place 8
schools 4, 6
smoke 4, 14
smoke detectors 12
sprinkler systems 12
stop, drop, and roll 16, 17
ways out 6, 8

Web Sites

Facts on Fire Safety for Kids, Parents, and Teachers
http://www.firefacts.org/

Fire Safety.gov for Kids
http://www.firesafety.gov/kids/flash.shtm

Sparky.org from the National Fire Protection Association
http://www.sparky.org